I0684422

WE WHISPER AND OTHER POEMS

SECOND EDITION

We Whisper

And Other Poems

Cedric L. Jones

Thespis Books | New York

Copyright © 2014, 2018 Cedric L. Jones

Thespis Books
New York, NY
www.ThespisBooks.com

Second Edition: July 2018

Jones, Cedric L., author

All rights reserved. This book or parts thereof may not be reproduced, stored in a retrieval system or transmitted in any form or by any means without the prior written permission of the publisher, or as permitted by U.S. Copyright law, except by a reviewer who may quote brief passages in a review to be printed in a newspaper, magazine, or blog- both print and online.

COVER PHOTO:

"Demonstrators marching in the street holding signs during the March on Washington, 1963" by Marion S. Trikosko, Aug. 28, 1963. Library of Congress, Prints & Photographs Division, Miscellaneous Items in High Demand, U.S. News & World Report Magazine Collection, [Reproduction Number LC-DIG-ds-04000; Call Number: LC-U9- 10344-14 [P&P]

Source: http://www.loc.gov/pictures/resource/ds.04000/

Section photography by Cedric L. Jones

ISBN: 1-7320357-1-7

ISBN-13: 978-1-7320357-1-3

FOR BILLY & JERMAINE

CONTENTS

*New additional poems

ONE

Desk at a New Jersey Yard Sale, 2013

Calendar

I see my mortality
Neatly printed in blocks
Counting up to a countdown
As I stretch and crackle and think,
What shall I learn today?

Autumn

Evening—
And all the leaves
Flutter down like torn dreams,
Brushing my face as they fall
And whispering
The passage of time.

Beneath my feet,
Twigs crackle like
Bones in early morning
And in the air hangs
That slight chill
Only comforted by sunlight
And not by the weight
Of a bothersome overcoat.

But oh,
The colors are glorious
And here and there
Reminders of my wild summer
Are strewn about:
White carnation petals,
Discarded royal jewels,
The pages of my blue journal—
All tokens from lost loves,
Reminders of friends past
In sands like an hour glass.

Alas, littered like broken glass.

Autumn has come.

I Am More

Grant me this favor—
Ask me my name
before you vow
to hate me.

I am more than
the dark brown
of my skin.
I am more than
the meat that swings
between my thighs.

I am more than
my Granddaddy's ashes.
I am more than
your Grandpappy's lies.

I am much more than
the names that
you call me,
and my name is
a great place to start.

'Cause if you
hide behind the me
that you've invented,
you'll never know
the contents of my heart!

Momma Once

Momma never understood
Why I shut up in a room,
Turned the lights down low
And read
Until I bled
Knowledge.

Momma didn't bother me.
She gave me eccentricity.
Momma used to let me be.

Momma once gave me
The things I need to survive—
A sharp tongue
A strong will
A weak eye
A heart for detail
And the pain of
Ages, ages hence.
Somehow, I found my confidence.

Momma once told me
That I shouldn't trust
Everyone I meet.

Momma once said
Someone would
Sweep me off my feet.

If Momma ever lied
It's so that I would be
A better man.

Momma,
Now I understand.

Momma taught me that there's
Nothing worth dying for
And everything worth living for
And everything worth crying for.

Momma once
Was the girl I was father to
And an idea I still cling to.

Momma didn't know me.
She'd never met a child like me.
Momma used to let me be.

O Momma!

I hope that you can see
The man that I have come to be
Because you chose to let me be me
And swallowed up in make believe.

Manners

Momma raised a gentleman
She didn't raise a sycophant
I'm serving you benevolence
If I should let you pass.

I may hold the door for you
You'd better thank me if I do
Or I might let that sucker slip
And knock you in the ass.

Wiser Man

I've been having such a grand life.
Every day outshined my last.
I've softly gathered truths
and time and courage
have amassed.

Each time I see a calendar
another year has passed.

Each time I gaze at the mirror
I'm different than before.

Each time I wake from slumbering
I want to slumber more

All in all my life is happy.
I don't live with much regret.
I've done what I can do
and what I haven't,
I forget.

So, farewell to my youth
for I am stronger
where I stand,
ready for the rest of life,
an older
Wiser Man.

First

When is it my turn?
It's always the women and the children
The challenged and the elderly
The one percent and the bourgeoisie
But what about me—
The overworked and marrow tired
The underemployed and uninspired
The used up and the undesired?

When is it my turn
To be first?

I'm bursting at the seams to know
When I shall be called to go
Before someone else?

Oh, yes—
To war on shores that are not mine
To rot in unemployment lines
A lineup where they'll say I did it!
A guest at Eunice Rivers' clinic.
To swing from trees as lassoed shade.
To test the drugs that gave us AIDS.

Who knows what's next?
It could be worse...

Never mind,
After all.
.
I don't want to be first.

I'm Alive

Mourn me
For the misery and pain
that you put me through
For the memories and grudgeries
I cling to
For my disappearing act
and my refusal to stay still
For the runaway inside me
and my strong, tenacious will.

Hate me
For the wondering and wandering
that stings you
For the silly little fantasies
I cling to
For the runaway inside me
that refuses still to call
knowing if I do
that I won't disappear at all.

But I'm alive!

Searching for direction
to my destiny
Knowing that you loved me
while you hated me.
I had to make a choice
And I chose to break free
to find some happy ending
and to learn who I should be.

I'm alive.

Leave me
As a photograph or an autograph
you cling to
As an oldies song from long ago
you sing to.
The Rhymer Boy without his toys
refuses to play nice
Bring me down before my time,
I'll have to leave you twice
to stay alive.

You Did Not

They taught me to tell
And I did
But you called me a liar
To please yourself
In front of those you
Wanted to please most.

So I crawled inside myself
Where I might have died
Because you lied
And I stayed alone
Cold
Just 2,920 days old.

And for the rest of my life.

You were supposed to
Believe me.

You were supposed
To protect the innocence
I held tight within my grasp
But you could not.

You were supposed to
Fight for me.

You were supposed
To shield me from
The cold fingers
That prodded me
But you did not.

You were supposed to
Teach me.

You were supposed to
Rock-a-bye me
And tell me I was a good boy
But you would not.

So when he came to me again
They taught me to lie
And that's exactly what I did
When I did as I was bid.

Because you were supposed
To love me.

The Sun

We're running for the sun
at breakneck speed,
bounding over hurdles
trying to meet the need
to be special.

I can't see how funny you run
'cause I'm elbows and backside
running for that sun.
I want to be
number one.

But will 15 minutes
be enough to warm you?

It doesn't matter,
I decide as I
run, run, run
jumping over pine trees
whizzing over lakes.
I shall run this race
'til I'm done.

I too
want my day in the sun.

CJ Was Here

I used to scratch
Into the marred wood
Of my desk

"CJ was here"

Too cowardly to
Write the full
Of my name
Lest I should get caught
Get in trouble
And be shamed.
These were the thoughts
That ran through my brain
Way back all those years
When

"CJ was here."

I used to be frightened
At recess
That some bully would
Catch up to me
And bloody my nose
Or break my bones.
I used to speak so softly
And spend all my time alone.

I had such little cheer
Way back then
When

"CJ was here."

But time has passed
And I've changed
And hardened like
Old gum beneath my desk.
One can't look
Into the past
Without having some regret.

I should have
Skipped more classes.
I should have
Failed more tests.
I should have
Scratched my full name.
I should have been bad those years
When

"CJ was here."

I should have
"Left my name to carry on."
I should have sang
Loud, rebellious songs.
I should have
Been more reckless
When allowed
The recklessness
Of youth.

I should have had
Less manners.
Hell, I should have
Had less couth.

I could have been
A real go-getter
If I'd known back then
That it gets better.

I imagine those desks
Piled high
In a graveyard
Alongside childhood fear
And what should have been.
I should take flowers
To mourn
Combinations for lockers
That have long ago
Been dismantled
And covered books,
Returned like new
That are no longer in print.

And on these
Long dark nights at home
When age can
Banish fear
I think back to a time
That should have been simple,
A time so far gone
But oh, so dear—
A time when

"CJ was here."

Life

I smile gracefully as you
Bray and kick your way
Around my world
Turning on me the bitter
Tooth of lost time,
Biting, scratching and
Kneeing me in the gut.
When I'm wrecked,
You're kind like a mother
Who bandages the knee.
You tuck me in
Warm and safe and blind
And I sleep smiling,
Knowing that tomorrow
You'll rip me
From the womb again.
Ah, life!
I'll attack you
Like a lover

Sick of holding back.

Lost Things

I'm done with mourning
lost things
like the sunglasses
I just left at the bank,
like my favorite ring
like love
and innocence
and the insecurity of youth.
I'll forget them
like my favorite ring.
I'm done with mourning
lost things.

TWO

American Stock Exchange, 2013

The Storm
November 28, 2017

Birds resist the wintertime,
gathering on rooftops in protest
while audacious squirrels stockpile nuts
resolutely, as if they have many a month to go,
the change of seasons a superstition,
rather than a mere fifty-three days
until the storm blows in.
Leaves bind to their trees,
and rain refuses to freeze.
Down below, we scuttle and puff,
icy with mistrust and anger and fear
at the change that's near.
We too refuse to batten down, succumb
to the daunting winter,
huddled around flaming effigies for heat.
We flock to the streets,
preparing to fight the coming storm.

Machine

I'm a disgruntled employee
of the master plan,
a working man
tinkering with the broken machine
and cursing to myself
as the wheels churn-jerk
in the rust of normality
—wherever the hell that lies
in the corporate agenda today.

With system failure everywhere
who wants to stay employed
in this crumbling factory
where there are no benefits
and my co-workers run
screaming mad in the street,
eliminating each other's positions
and downsizing us
to the unsophisticated creeps
that we are?

What work is man.

Money grubbing CEOs
snarl death from pulpits
dripping blood,
while nuclear ants
invade the company picnic and
laborers prostitute themselves
to the mission statement of destruction.

We are asleep at the wheel
of an unraveling society,
delivering nothing.

I punch and scratch and kick
this damned machine
that won't produce.

But oh, what work is man
so happy in his noose.

Dirty Nails

Dirty Nails.
We all have them,
but what do we
use them to do?
Write poetry,
play piano,
pour the drinks
that make men soar,
or make them dirty
even more
by tilling soil,
or painting walls,
or leading horses
into stalls?

Some dirty nails
define life
as we claw into existence
and scratch our names
into the earth.
We don our kid gloves
to hide our dirty nails.
For, no one wants
to see the labor,
but everyone
wants to taste the fruit.

Mask

You're spinning around
Like a two-sided jack,
A smile to my face
And a knife to my back.

I love the way you look at me
With your painted face
And smile so fake.

But, the soul behind your eyes
Is lacking.
It seems to me
Your mask is cracking.

It's easy to see
That your camaraderie
Has the ring
Of a circus attraction.

You're kind to me
Where people can see
But, be careful
Of your ringleader acting.
With one mistake,
Your mask is cracking.

I'm not put at ease
By the smile on your face
As you sell reparations
And credits to race
While swearing,
"One love!"
From your station above
For, racist is as racist does.

Yes, the soul behind your eyes
Is lacking.
You've stumbled
And your mask is cracking.

Box of Rock
(Ode to a User)

Silly addict.

Who do you think you're fooling
with your tales of pomp and glory?
I've already heard this story,
and it wasn't even yours.

You're forgetting
who you are,
—a polluted,
crack rock star,
a charismatic speedball
with a tendency to lie
and, for every dime
that's missing
there's a sweeping alibi.

You've got a sweet tooth
for the candy-*caine*
and it's a shame
but you must have tripped
and bruised your brain
that day you crossed me.
See, you're forgetting
who I am
—the one who used to
give a damn
before your
gutter glitter healer.
So, save that back talk
for your dealer.

You're flaky, Mr. Snowman,
a dragon chasing mess.
Get a grip
on that rent check,
and not that spoon
around your neck,
and stop whizzing 'round
through snow lights
in a house
built from a deck.

I don't like you here this way.
I like you when you go away
and let me detox
with civility
from your stupidity.
You embarrass me.

Friends like you
must share their woe.
I wish you'd
take your bag
and blow,
and stop draining me
of all my good intentions
with all your interventions.

You're a jinx,
a bad invention.

You're chasing floppy socks,
and thinking like a box of rock.

Jackass and Co.

Piles of time cards that never end
like work days on a calendar.

Crass boisterous voices of men
loud with stupidity and bravado
on whom self reflection
is lost between the file cabinets
and will be useless
when found years later.

Puppet masters who control lives
and livelihoods
from a conference table
piled with documents
that mean nothing to men
who must feed children.

These ass-clowns are
aping the actions
of real businessmen
they've copied from a machine.

They gather around
that copy me machine
bragging of their wealth and
following the lead of
a drunken pied piper.

And me in my cubicle
powerless to save the people,
the human resource,
from these frenzied ass-clowns
and the jackass who leads them.

Sprout

Said the bean sprout
to the soil,
  "Get outta my way man,
I got somewhere to be!"

And he pushed and pushed
and pushed himself free.

He reached for the sun
and twisted in the wind and said,
  "Howdy-do?"
To his bean sprout friends.

For all o're the field
a gathering commenced
of nodding bean sprouts
so happy to be free.

Peace

Let's be the rain
Softly showering
The wildflower meadow
Evenly and all the same
—as in equality and peace.

The Change We Want to See

Daddy didn't like the world,
He couldn't take the strife.
So, Daddy took complete control.
Once night, he took his life.

Sister had a boyfriend,
He's a mean and hateful man.
One day, he shot her to the ground
And took baby when he ran.

Momma's doing prison time
But she can't settle down.
She's haunted every hour
By the two young boys she drowned.

Brother had a funny walk,
Some called it a sashay.
On the night he died
They tried to beat the gay away.

This world is spinning madly,
Spinning madly off in space.
We're looking for a hero
Who can save the human race.

But we should look no further
Than each other—
You and me.
To find it in our hearts
To be the change we want to see.

Gather It Calmly

When the winds of life
have blown you about
and you're left with debris
from a storm of doubt,
just gather it calmly.
Gather it calmly.

When tears of heartache
have rendered you blind
and close to the danger
of losing your mind,
just gather it calmly.
Gather it calmly.

When you've saved and scraped
but still need much more
and your back is so bent
—too numb to be sore;
You've worked 'til you're broken
and dead on your feet

When there seems no chance
of making ends meet,
there is nothing like grace
to conquer defeat!
So, gather it calmly.
Gather it calmly.

Yes, gather it calmly.
Oh, very calmly.

THREE

God's Image Poster, NYC Gay Pride 2012

Savior

Christ is coming
and he doesn't want to hear
any of your damned excuses
for what happened at
Egypt, Auschwitz, Wounded Knee,
Selma, The Mississippi Delta.
He grabs the priest
by the collar
and throws him from the pulpit
and breathes fire
over a self-righteous congregation
gathered around the auction block.
We make him sick.
He spits the words with fervor
and washes light into our souls.
Language jumbles and we are color blind.
We stand naked
in a brand new Eden
feeling stupid
for all the things we've done.
The savior doesn't save.
He leaves us to reflect.

How Dare You?

There is a time
for everything under Heaven—
a time to laugh, a time to weep
a time to dare.

I'm asking,
how dare you
judge my spirituality?

Don't fill my soul
full of scorn
when I am spirit free
and Heaven born.

How dare you
answer before you ask me?

How dare you
drench me before a storm?

I look for a world
of understanding
as harmonious and flowing
as song.

Until you can tell me
what is absolutely right,
how dare you
tell me what is wrong?

I'm angry that you think I'm angry.
I've sorry because you think I'm sad.
But if I follow you
in blindness
then I must be raving mad!

There is a time
for everything under Heaven
and it's time you understand
that it's not right to
take away my freedom
because I love another man.

How dare you
assume I'm religious
and tell me you'll
pray for me?

You assume that
I need your salvation
when what I need
is democracy.

How dare you
label me before
you know my contents?

How dare you
label my difference
as odd?

How dare you
think you have the answers?

How dare you
speak for my God?

Don't answer.

O Humanity!

O Humanity!
Turn your eyes from Heaven
toward your fellow man.
See him humbled, bruised and broken
where he stands,
scarred by the fallen branches
of a singed family tree.
There in ruin, stands a man
akin to me.

Journey (Apollyon)

I will go to war with the long sword of
my mouth, made strong by the feast of
the hidden manna.
—white pebble
And I am the morning star before the
fall, but no one will take my crown of
Seven Flames.
I saw the Lamb of God and bound its
wounds as it whispered from the scrolls
and I set out with my long sword, my
flaming crown and my rainbow horse.
I put on a white robe, held fast to the
wind and sailed.
I descended on the 144 thousand in
need.
Woe be to men, who tell me I shall die.
They speak with the acid tongue of the
devil,
And there is only one kind of lie.

Don't Knock

Of the one hundred and forty-four thousand
who will make it
you think that I am none
but I know I am the one
who will find my Heaven.

So don't knock on my door no more!

If you pray against me
then well,
what you send to me
shall return
times 3, times 7
and send you straight to hell
so don't you dare
ring my bell

And don't knock on my door no more!

If you stop and take a look
between the covers of that book
that you're dealing like a crook
you just might bear Witness to

The Genocide
The Homicide
The Suicide
The Hate-ocide
and know
that you're to blame.

Ain't that a shame?

It's the reason
your numbers are few,
the things
you do and don't do
while you judge from
a sacred temple
built of lies
in your exclusive
house of flies
where blood don't splatter
and the Lord don't matter.

So,
Shoo Fly!
Don't bother me!

Knocking at my door
ringing up my phone
disturbing me with
righteousness
here at my own home.

Don't knock at my door no more!

God War

Goddess come down and
Deliver us from the rest
Of humanity!

And she heard our cry and did try
But was crushed by the patriarchy
As mankind warred
With the sword
Of misogyny
And slew the world
In the name of God.

But we who know
It's a show
Find it odd
That you destroy what you have
In the name of the Father
While you let down
And tie down
Your mothers and daughters

And teach moral justice
With hypocrite breath
As your God and his God
Both fight to the death.

It's no wonder you create
God in your own image.
You need your
Mascot to witness
The scrimmage.

The New God

I need a God
But I don't want to kneel
To one
You've used up like napkins
Over a meal.

I want a fresh God.
So, I must either
Invent one
Or resurrect those of old
Despite the goal
To sacrifice them
To fantasy.

Your God is convenient
While my God shall be bold,
Cunning, wise, stunning
Legendary, fierce!

And no matter
Where we come from
Where we're going
What we're doing
Or what we've done,
The New God
Shall love the lot of us,
Each and every one.

Suffer Me to Live (20:13)

I stand before a jeering crowd.
While you shout of religion
Your hatred is loud.
Your morals are at stake.
You burn me at the stake

For thou shalt not
Suffer me to live.

I run through the reeds
Toward freedom,
Away from the shackles
And cotton, and
Leather stings my back.
There is no turning back

For thou shalt not
Suffer me to live.

I stand at the forked road
Of liberty or death.
I cannot keep my step.
I cannot catch my breath.
My determination is strong.
The current of the hose is strong

For thou shalt not
Suffer me to live.

And yet, I live
To stand for what is right.
We the people demand what's right
Because we've learned to fight
And we've just begun to fight.

For,
My spirit
Thou shalt not kill.

Let Us Go

So you're calling me a sinner
With your list of human crimes
Selling monkeyshines contrition,
And tall tales of ending times.

You better let my people go.

You think that we don't notice
That you've got the lion's share,
While we're left with no salvation
And an empty hope and prayer.

You'd better open up those gates
And let us go.

So you say that we should pray
For the sick and for the dying.
What they need is better health care,
Not the magic beans they're buying.

You better let my people go.

You medicate with blindness
But it's not so hard to see
Through your acts of desperation
And your false divinity.

You'd better open up those gates
And let us go.

Go on and open
Up those gates
Cause you're running
Out of time.
Stop turning fear
Into religion
And selling faith
Like it was wine.

With your mouth
That smells of brimstone
And your soul
As dark as night,
You've got us shackled
In the prison
Of your wrong Religious Right.

Go on and open
Up those gates
Let us go!
Let us go!

You better open up those gates
And let us go.

FOUR

Liberty Takes a Break, Times Square 2018

11 O'clock

I try to ignore
the onslaught of racism
streaming like feces
from the shit-show called the nightly news.
I try to be zen
but mostly I'm
tired and frightened,
disgusted, insulted
and thoroughly confused.

Enough

You've ripped from me
my ancestry
both Black and Native proud.

Now you profile me.
It hurts in that
cavity inside where
something is missing
that I can't identify.

Every time you
trace your roots
it is a slap in my face,
for I have been uprooted.

Your family tree
still bears the fibers
of the ropes
that strangled mine.

Today,
you treat me like a thief
and profile me
in the street and heap
upon me the hate
taught to you.

When will anyone care
about the content
of my character?

When will that be enough?

We Whisper

We grunt against obscurity
stomping on the pavement
trying to leave a footprint
that won't wash away tomorrow
when this is yesterday.

Words are forever
and mighty.
Statues—
they crumble
and make useless noise.

But we whisper.

We whisper our woes
in the dank hulls
of slave ships
bound for a history
we can't escape.

We whisper despair
on the long trail
from Carolina to Arkansas.

We whisper hope
through tear gas
from Selma to Montgomery.

We whisper through
the jeers of the mob
in Little Rock.

We whisper
in and out of doors,
we whisper
on the war swept shores.

We whisper in silence.
We whisper in truth.

And the whispers through time
grow so loud
we shout!

We tell our tales
so they cannot
be forgotten.

We talk to
those who will listen,
but we whisper
to those who will tell.

Cherokee Rose

Golden
Like tears scattered
On hardened Southern soil
The Cherokee Rose is blooming
With Pride.

Need

We race past the disenfranchised
And the places that they roam
To adopt a third world country's child
Somewhere, online, at home.

Most of ours can barely read
Or find themselves in desperate need.
It's amazing how our hearts can bleed
For someone we don't know.

Tuesday

I'm angry like
the time my Mother
threw out my favorite jeans
because they got too tight.

That's why they were
my favorite jeans.

I'm angry like
the time I had to
stay after school
for something
I didn't do.

Or wear those sin-ugly
affordable shoes.

Or the time I had
to break my cookie in two
'cause sharing is the thing to do.

But what do you do
when you're trapped
and you can't spank Momma
and teachers don't get detention
and there's no discipline
for the disciplinarian?

It seems I can't do
anything about anything.

Like that time
I was called a liar
for telling the truth,
or the time the tooth fairy
took my money
and my tooth!

Now,
it's Tuesday,
and I'm going to stand in line
for this voting booth
even if it takes all day.

And I'm gonna
hold my breath
and stomp my feet
and pull that lever
until I get my way.

First Day of School

On the first morning
Adults are as the shrill bell,
"No Negroes allowed!"
Her children will know freedom.
She doesn't know that today.

We the People

We the people
Are waiting patiently
For you to get it right

For when you won't
Take away our rights
Like a thief in the night

Because you are afraid
That there's a threat
To what is White.

We the people
Are afraid of another
Forced internment

That what happened
In the recent past is not
Is not a good deterrent

That you'll
Gather us together
For expressing our endearment.

We the people
Are still trying
To find our pedigrees

From when you
Took away our lands
And you forced us to retreat

Or when you took us
From our lands
And our true identities.

We the people
Are still hoping for you to
Clear your head

For when you
Won't take forever
To see what lies ahead.

So many fight for freedom
But only find it
When they're dead.

And we do wonder
If the world
Will ever be one.

And we wonder if
There will be
A world left
When you are done.

And we wonder if,
Right now, there is
A place for us at all

When every time we
Start out walking
You knock us down to crawl.

And we do care
If you love us.
We're the ones
Who built this land.

So, stop giving us
The finger and try
Giving us a hand.

But
We, the people
Understand that our
Nation is still learning.

It's because we've come so far
That we know
The tide is turning.

We the people
Want an end to all the hate
And mass confusion.

We the people
Are still waiting
To share your closed communion

And,
We the people
Are waiting patiently
To form a perfect union.

Sanford

In the afterglow
Of the evening news
We are shocked
By the Sanford defeat.

But why?

It harkens still
To Emmett Till.

It's haunting
How history repeats.

Enslaved

Don't call me that nasty racist word
With the same inflection you say brother
And expect me to answer you with glee.
You've just insulted me
By calling me the very thing
We have strived for hundreds of years
Not to be—

Enslaved.

African America

We demand to be called
African American in board rooms
But we call each other
Slave names in the street.

We are complete and total strangers
At the crossroads
Where assimilation and militancy meet.

You're too quick to call me names
Because you do not like
The way that I walk.
I'm too quick to check my wallet
Because I do not like
The way that you talk.

African America,
God shed his grace on thee.

Can a Southern brother
And a Northern cousin
Sit down and have a talk
Or a cry about how
It feels to be kicked
To the ground where
Other men walk,
And how self-respect
Can be sold and bought
But is worth more than
A street reputation
Or the two bucks it costs
To download
A song filled with degradation?

We, the people
Of Black Pride
And soulful power,
Now is the time
And now is the hour to
Take a moment of silence
And respect the Old Souls
That worked and died to
Build our nation
With a heritage so rich
It drips down like blood
To fertilize even the stubborn
Red clay of Georgia
Used to bake bricks
In soul-fire,
And carried with arms made strong
By the weight of chains
…and change.

And still.

We are complete and total strangers
At the crossroads
Where getting by and getting over merge.

We have filled our cups
With courage, but
We still don't have the nerve
To take a sip,
To take a step,
To move forward
And drop bad habits
Like feet on dusty roads
Leading from darkness to light.

African America,
God shed his grace on thee.

And,
The plantation owners snicker
And slap each other on the back
And spit as they exchange $2 bills
And laugh and say,
I told you so.

We demand to be called
African American in board rooms
But we call each other
Slave names in the street.

We are complete and total strangers
At the crossroads
Where emancipation and slavery repeat.

Words of Hate

Just because
you think you know
doesn't mean you do.

Those things you said
at the dinner table
in the office
at the store
in school

about the news

fell on ears
that suffer
because you

speak that way.

Realize there are
differences
all around you

and stop
filling the air with
words of hate.

Terror in the Homeland

The terrorist threat is looming
says the News at Eleven
that boys will be good ole boys
who'd rather run me up a tree
than let me choke on a piece
of the American Pie
as they lie
to create a New Republic
White nation under God
in a stash house with a steeple
built from the bones
of We the People.

There's some distorting
in the reporting
of the devil
going down to Georgia, y'all.

Somebody better make the call
to the Black man and the White lady
on the T.V. who kee-kee
about democracy
while the separatists
are stalking me.

Tell them
there's a problem, we
can't hunker down
and batten hatches.
There's nowhere to hide
when the insurgents are inside.

They're not holed up
in the desert
but marching down the street
in dusty sheets and pillow cases
stomping progress
with their feet.

We need more
security within the homeland
so that a Black man
can go on being a living man
or else be struck down
where he stands
like Mr. Evers
and all the others.

Like the Three Wise Men
killed near Meridian
or the four little angels
who'll never sing again.

I fear this is the end,
as though they're stockpiling
ignorance and gunpowder
but the two don't mix so well
and opposing politics will
spark and blow us all to hell.

So, I'm saving up water
for the Judgment Day
when we'll all get burned
by the KKK.

For Just a Little While

Try to understand just a little
For just a little while.

Have you ever been in love
But not allowed to love?

It's like a mountain
Not allowed to touch the sky

Or an ocean that's not allowed to
Wet the shore…

Or a fire without a flame.

Have you ever known
The kind of love
That is two reaches away—

One reaching out
The other reaching in

And not knowing which way
To reach yourself?

Have you?

Try to understand just a little
For just a little while.

Indian Giver

Thanksgiving Day 2016

Oh, say can you see
by the dawn's early light
the Natives falling down
at Standing Rock
in a centuries old fight
against oil in the water
and blood on the ground
while Capitol Hill is gleaming
and devoid of sound?

We watch with turkey stained breath
to see if our government will
kneel down to a corporation
like a virgin to a god
or stand and Ghost Dance
before a militia that would rather
bust head than break bread.

And you ask Little Timmy,
"What is Thanksgiving?"
Without any guise in
his little blue eyes, he says,
"It's the day the Pilgrims and the Indians
made peace and shared a feast."

What will it take to placate
America's great state of hate?

Will federalism rise and deliver,
or choose to snatch more indigenous land
like a greedy "Indian giver"?

Downfall

November 2016

We sway on the precipice of downfall.
Megalomaniacs will torch the tree
Of knowledge with their dragon breath and gall
And slay the eagle of democracy.

Jester's dance is merely a distraction.
We shake our heads but turn to late to see
Rising of a neo-fascist faction
That comes for him and her and you and me.

Yesteryear's atrocities forgotten?
"The sins were purged, the guilty have atoned,"
So we say while social grace is trodden.
Let's not forget the fall of mighty Rome.

The fear of repetition we deride.
How soon before we turn to genocide?

I Am Brown

I am brown like hard liquor. I sting and I burn

Terracotta like the ground
Brown like slavery.
Darker against cotton than dirt, twisted in a sun
that's hotter-than-a-motherland

Brown like leather, work-worn
and wearied and tanned
Like the blood-stained soil of the Southern-land
I am brown like 40 acres and a mule

Brown like my Momma, dark like my Daddy
I am brown like a penny, valued like a penny,
spent like a penny, discarded like a penny

As brown as the cross at Calvary
I am brown like the bark on a hanging tree

     But, as brown as I am
     I am still red and white and blue.

Do not treat me as less American than you.

Sequined Wings

I got faith, you got faith
All God's Children got faith.
But I lost all my religion
Trying to keep amazing grace.

I got doubts, you got doubts
All God's Children got doubts.
Gonna go on down to Laramie
To see what doubt's about.

I got pride, you got pride
All God's Children got pride.
I'm marching down to Christopher Street.
To keep my pride alive.

I got voice, you got voice
All God's Children got voice.
I'm gonna sing out loud,
Dance and be proud
That it's a blessing,
Not a choice.

And all y'all
Who's falling down
And shouting out to God,
And talking 'bout Heaven
And Heavenly living
And all the while
You're fibbing and killing —
Stop hiding behind your
Damned religion.

I got wings, you got wings
All God's Children got sequined wings!
We should be proud and march and sing
And wave our flag
And exchange our rings.
We are famous for a million things.

Yes, all The Children got
Sequined wings.

In the News

I'm a come over there
With my NYC flare
And plug up that hole
Where your heart should be.
Why are you constantly
Jerking around
And beating down
People like me?

It's giving me the blues
What I see in the news.

You turned on me
When I bucked your
Idea of normality
Down across that
Mason-Dixon line
Where you punished me with
Hate Crimes.

It's giving me the blues
What I see in the news.

Gunshots and bleeding—
Everybody screams,
But I just can't turn away.
It's making me weep
How we die in the street
And it just gets worse every day.

Some psychologists say
It's because you might sway
To the side of us,
Crave your own sex like
The rest of us
And you get so vexed
To be one of us
That you lash out fast
To be rid of us.
But getting rid of us
Won't make you go away.
So, live for tomorrow,
And stop killing yourself today.

It's giving me the blues
What I see in the news.

Breakfast

I want to start my day
as normal people do—

I make breakfast
I turn on the news.

But it ain't new anymore—
another Black man was shot at the corner of
Enough! and *What for?*

I eat my heart out with a fork
and splash juice in my eyes,
plug up my ears with bacon and fat,
fall to my knees and beg like it's bedtime.

"Please don't let me die today!"

Then, I rise and put the breakfast
things away.

Hate Crime

From high above
I see myself
jerked
from the vehicle,
thrown to the pavement.

Epithet! Epithet!
Slur! Slur!

The lawyer will tell me
there is no
Hate Crime Law
in South Carolina.

I feel that
in the moments
you bash me.

This is What Happens!

"See!"
You told the people,

"This is what happens
when you turn *gay!"*

But then the genocide
that you devised
began to blow your way.

First you told the world,
about the gay man's cancer!
But, when your neighbors fell
you couldn't give
them any answers.

This is what happens
when you go to a sword fight
with a snake.
That little bastard
will turn around and
strike you in your face.

And in the Senate
you try to make your actions
seem defensible.

*"We only used it on
the lowly lot of people
deemed dispensable."*

Like the blacks in Tuskegee
who died without a fight
or the poor slave women
who were sliced up in the night.
Let's remember WWII
and what the Nazis
did to Jews
or those people
of the yesteryear
you gave those blankets to.

This is what happens
when you mess with our heads.

You bade us come
for medical trials
and 33 million ended up dead
when we took your experiments
from your labs
to our neighborhoods
to our loved ones
to our homes
to our beds.

For hundreds of years
you've been causing devastation
as your germ warfare and
experimentation
is killing nation upon nation.

Civilizations crumble
when your conspiracy is flawed.

This is what happens
when you start playing God.

Pink Sheets and
Rainbow Hoods

Hey Miss Thing,

I hope I don't offend
with my cappuccino skin
but you've got a lot of brass
trying to read
my proud Black ass.

Making reference to
the slavery of me?
Honey please!
You'd better take off
that pink sheet
and watch me drop
these here truth beads.

You're marching around
in your pink sheet
and rainbow hood.
You'd better do what's good
for the Gay-borhood
and treat a brother
like you should.

Don't treat me like
the Right-Wing
who wish I'd go away
'cause I sing
my loud gay anthem
no matter what they say.

Don't treat me like
the Left-Wing
who use me like a crutch
but clutch their pearls
and lock their doors
If my Black is butch.

Treat me like an equal
for, this is an equal fight—
To be housed, employed and wed
To be equal in our rights

To be safe from harm in the street
To protect our freedom there.
It's an equal dream we dream.
It's an equal pain we share.

We have survived
the tyranny and scrutiny,
religion and hypocrisy
to build our sickening legacy.
So, honey when you look at me
see pride and strong tenacity.
Ms. Marsha P. was Black like me.

So, remember Stonewall
and don't stone y'all.
Do you get what I mean?
I'm a sassy Black queen
who totes a heavy load
and though it sparkles
and I'm Fierce,
that racist vibe upsets me
and those nasty words still pierce.

Especially from you
for, I should have brother there
and not just another White man
too bigoted to care.

But, hey
we're all just human,
fools against our will.
In our cause we stand,
but apart
we're standing still.

Yet, this movement
shall move forward
and we'll break free
as we all should.

When you take off
that damned pink sheet
and lay down
that rainbow hood.

It's a Shame

You cling
to the religion
thrust upon you by
our old oppressors
and wield it
as you dub me
Satan's child.

O Black people!

Perhaps it's been
a while since

we were
hosed down in the street
victims of hate and deceit
in our fight for democracy.

It's a shame
you don't accept me.

It's a shame
you treat me this way.

It's a shame you say
I'm a waste of a Black man

just because I'm gay.

We are the Americans

We alight on the shores
Each one with some kind of hope
For some kind of freedom.
We are pilgrims and prisoners
Natives and slaves
Explorers and conquistadors.
We are the Americans.

We work side by side
And against each other
To build one indivisible nation,
But we work.
Ours is the mixed blood of
Warrior and pacifist
Shaman and priest,
Peasant and king.
We are the Americans.

We have the heartbeat of the bear
And the wingspan of the eagle
But the flutter
And softness of the dove.
We will grab you with
Our eagle talons
In our campaigns
And demonstrations.

We are the arbiter of truth
And the leader of nations,
Strong in our convictions
And fierce in our relations.
Our justice
Is the justice of legend
From shining sea to shining sea.

We are the Americans
And we are free.

Goodbye Oppression!

I've been whispering
all these years
but now it's time for me to shout—

Oppression,
pack your things,
leave your keys
and get out!

No!
Take your keys
'cause I'm changing the locks.

Forward your mail,
book a hotel
notify your friends and what not.

Damn!
I've been living with you
for far too long.

I don't even like your friends
your choice in
newspapers, news stations, magazines,
or songs!

Oppression,
you have beleaguered me
and kept me down.

All I wanted was to believe
there was freedom
to be found.

I was down so low
you had me thinking
I was better off dead.

I had to get you
Out of my house
Out of my heart
Out of my soul
Out of my head!

Oppression,
I can't reconcile with you
but I can change my name
from *Mr. Left Behind*
to *Mr. I'm Too Through With You*

Close the joint account
I had with you—

Throw away the lies
I got from you—

Dry the tired eyes
that cried for you—

Heal from all the pain
I had with you!

Oppression,
I thought that you were
the only life
I could ever have.

That's because what
I saw on the news each day
seemed so bad.

But I simply had to
look inside of me
to find my way—

So what I didn't
have yesterday,
I'll have tomorrow
'cause I said good-bye
to you today!

Oppression,
my head and my heart
are so much lighter
since I've realized
I've always been a fighter.

I have so much joy
now that I have
learned life's lessons
and I can finally say to you

Goodbye Oppression!

ABOUT THE AUTHOR

Cedric L. Jones writes poetry, drama, and the occasional comedy sketch. He is the author of three books of poetry, *I Wear the Colour Green, We Whisper and Other Poems,* and *Today, I Found This Rose.* He was named the 2000 Emerald Theatre Best Play Award recipient, as well as a finalist for the Manhattan Theatre Source 12th Annual EstroGenius Festival. His short plays *Verses* and *Trouble in Paradise* were performed in Manhattan as part of the 10th Annual Midtown International Play Festival under the collected title *Bible Stories.* In addition to writing, he enjoys acting and performing as the vocalist with the jazz trio *Mister Diva & The Gents.*

ABOUT THESPIS

Legend has it that the poet Thespis was the first person to step away from the Greek Chorus to assume a dramatic character. In the role of Dionysus, God of wine and theater, he became the first actor, or *thespian.*

www.ingramcontent.com/pod-product-compliance
Lightning Source LLC
Chambersburg PA
CBHW051842170626
46807CB00003B/1302